Moments We Share

A Father & Son Journal

George McMann

Copyright

© Copyright 2025 George McMann

All rights reserved. No part of this publication may be used or reproduced without permission of George McMann.

Published by:

PANTHERA PUBLISHING
PANTHERAPUBLISHING.COM
STUART, FLORIDA

OUR SPECIAL JOURNAL: ADVENTURES OF DAD & I

A special place to record memories, adventures, and fun times together.

[Insert a special photo(s) here]

ABOUT US

Dad's Info:

- Name: _____

- Favorite Hobbies: _____

- Favorite Food: _____

- Fun Fact: _____

Son's Info:

- Name: _____

- Favorite Hobbies: _____

- Favorite Food: _____

- Fun Fact: _____

[Insert a father-son photo here]

BUCKET LIST OF ADVENTURES

[ ] Build a fort

[ ] Go fishing

[ ] Ride bikes together

[ ] Camp in the backyard

[ ] Fly a kite

[ ] Play a sport together

[ ] Have a movie night

[ ] Bake cookies

[ ] Visit a zoo or aquarium

[ ] Do a science experiment together

[Insert a fun activity photo here]

WEEKLY CHALLENGE

Dad's Challenge for Son: _____

_____

Son's Challenge for Dad: _____

_____

How did we do? (Draw or write about it!)

_____

_____

[Insert a challenge-related photo here]

MEMORY PAGE

This week, we had fun doing _____.

_____

 (Draw or paste a photo here!)

[Insert a memory photo here]

JOKE & RIDDLE CORNER

Dad's joke: _____

_____

_____

Son's joke:

_____

_____

_____

A riddle for next time: _____

_____

_____

[Insert a fun or silly photo here]

STORY TIME

Once upon a time, we went on an adventure...

(Write a story together!)

_____

_____

_____

_____

_____

_____

_____

_____

_____

[Insert an adventure photo here]

GRATITUDE PAGE

Today, I am thankful for...

Dad: _____

Son: _____

[Insert a gratitude-related photo here]

ADVICE FROM DAD

Dad writes a life lesson or advice:

_____

_____

_____

_____

Son writes what he thinks about it:

_____

_____

_____

[Insert a wisdom-themed photo here]

FUTURE MESSAGES

Dad's letter to Son:

_____

_____

_____

_____

Son's letter to Dad:

_____

_____

_____

[Insert a sentimental photo here]

BIBLE VERSE DISCUSSION

Bible Verse of the Week:

(Write a verse here)

_____

_____

_____

What does this verse mean to us?

Dad's thoughts: _____

_____

_____

_____

_____

Son's thoughts: _____

_____

_____

_____

_____

How can we apply this in our daily lives?

_____

_____

_____

_____

_____

_____

_____

_____

[Insert an inspirational photo here]

🚀 FUN ADVENTURE TOGETHER!

📅 **Date:** _____

🎯 **Our Mission Today:**
What exciting thing did we do together?
_____
_____

😃 🎉 **The Best Part:**
What was the most fun or memorable moment?
_____
_____

📷 ✏️ **Picture Time!**
(Draw a picture of our adventure!)

🤝 💙 **Teamwork Moment:**
How did we help each other today?
_____
_____
_____

15

🙏 👏 **Thank You, God, For:**

One thing we're grateful for today:

_____

_____

☀️ **What We Learned:**

Did we discover something new?

_____

_____

_____

➡️ **Next Adventure Idea:**

What do we want to do together next time?

_____

_____

WEEKLY CHALLENGE

Dad's Challenge for Son: _____

_____

Son's Challenge for Dad: _____

_____

How did we do? (Draw or write about it!)

_____

_____

[Insert a challenge-related photo here]

MEMORY PAGE

This week, we had fun doing _____.

_____

   (Draw or paste a photo here!)

[Insert a memory photo here]

JOKE & RIDDLE CORNER

Dad's joke: _____

_____

_____

Son's joke:

_____

_____

_____

A riddle for next time: _____

_____

_____

[Insert a fun or silly photo here]

STORY TIME

Once upon a time, we went on an adventure...

(Write a story together!)

_____

_____

_____

_____

_____

_____

_____

_____

_____

[Insert an adventure photo here]

GRATITUDE PAGE

Today, I am thankful for…

Dad: _____

Son: _____

[Insert a gratitude-related photo here]

ADVICE FROM DAD

Dad writes a life lesson or advice:

_____

_____

_____

_____

Son writes what he thinks about it:

_____

_____

_____

[Insert a wisdom-themed photo here]

FUTURE MESSAGES

Dad's letter to Son:

_____

_____

_____

_____

Son's letter to Dad:

_____

_____

_____

[Insert a sentimental photo here]

BIBLE VERSE DISCUSSION

Bible Verse of the Week:

(Write a verse here)

_____

_____

_____

What does this verse mean to us?

Dad's thoughts: _____

_____

_____

_____

_____

Son's thoughts: _____

_____

_____

_____

_____

How can we apply this in our daily lives?

_____

_____

_____

_____

_____

_____

_____

_____

[Insert an inspirational photo here]

🚀 FUN ADVENTURE TOGETHER!

📅 **Date:** _____

🎯 **Our Mission Today:**
What exciting thing did we do together?
_____

_____

😃 🎉 **The Best Part:**
What was the most fun or memorable moment?
_____

_____

📷 ✏️ **Picture Time!**
(Draw a picture of our adventure!)

🤝 💙 **Teamwork Moment:**
How did we help each other today?
_____

_____

_____

🙏 🙌 **Thank You, God, For:**

One thing we're grateful for today:

_____

_____

☀️ **What We Learned:**

Did we discover something new?

_____

_____

_____

➡️ **Next Adventure Idea:**

What do we want to do together next time?

_____

_____

WEEKLY CHALLENGE

Dad's Challenge for Son: _____

_____

Son's Challenge for Dad: _____

_____

How did we do? (Draw or write about it!)

_____

_____

[Insert a challenge-related photo here]

MEMORY PAGE

This week, we had fun doing _____.

_____

 (Draw or paste a photo here!)

[Insert a memory photo here]

JOKE & RIDDLE CORNER

Dad's joke: _____

_____

_____

Son's joke:

_____

_____

_____

A riddle for next time: _____

_____

_____

[Insert a fun or silly photo here]

STORY TIME

Once upon a time, we went on an adventure...

(Write a story together!)

_____

_____

_____

_____

_____

_____

_____

_____

_____

[Insert an adventure photo here]

GRATITUDE PAGE

Today, I am thankful for…

Dad: _____

Son: _____

[Insert a gratitude-related photo here]

ADVICE FROM DAD

Dad writes a life lesson or advice:

_____

_____

_____

_____

Son writes what he thinks about it:

_____

_____

_____

[Insert a wisdom-themed photo here]

FUTURE MESSAGES

Dad's letter to Son:

_____

_____

_____

_____

Son's letter to Dad:

_____

_____

_____

[Insert a sentimental photo here]

BIBLE VERSE DISCUSSION

Bible Verse of the Week:

(Write a verse here)

_____

_____

_____

What does this verse mean to us?

Dad's thoughts: _____

_____

_____

_____

_____

Son's thoughts: _____

_____

_____

_____

_____

How can we apply this in our daily lives?

_____

_____

_____

_____

_____

_____

_____

_____

[Insert an inspirational photo here]

🚀 FUN ADVENTURE TOGETHER!

📅 **Date:** _____

🎯 **Our Mission Today:**
What exciting thing did we do together?
_____

_____

😃 🎉 **The Best Part:**
What was the most fun or memorable moment?
_____

_____

📷 ✏️ **Picture Time!**
(Draw a picture of our adventure!)

🤝 💙 **Teamwork Moment:**
How did we help each other today?
_____

_____

_____

🙏 👐 **Thank You, God, For:**

One thing we're grateful for today:

_____

_____

🌟 **What We Learned:**

Did we discover something new?

_____

_____

_____

➡️ **Next Adventure Idea:**

What do we want to do together next time?

_____

_____

WEEKLY CHALLENGE

Dad's Challenge for Son: _____

_____

Son's Challenge for Dad: _____

_____

How did we do? (Draw or write about it!)

_____

_____

[Insert a challenge-related photo here]

MEMORY PAGE

This week, we had fun doing _____.

_____

   (Draw or paste a photo here!)

[Insert a memory photo here]

JOKE & RIDDLE CORNER

Dad's joke: _____

_____

_____

Son's joke:

_____

_____

_____

A riddle for next time: _____

_____

_____

[Insert a fun or silly photo here]

STORY TIME

Once upon a time, we went on an adventure...

(Write a story together!)

_____

_____

_____

_____

_____

_____

_____

_____

[Insert an adventure photo here]

GRATITUDE PAGE

Today, I am thankful for...

Dad: _____

Son: _____

[Insert a gratitude-related photo here]

ADVICE FROM DAD

Dad writes a life lesson or advice:

_____

_____

_____

_____

Son writes what he thinks about it:

_____

_____

_____

[Insert a wisdom-themed photo here]

FUTURE MESSAGES

Dad's letter to Son:

_____

_____

_____

_____

Son's letter to Dad:

_____

_____

_____

[Insert a sentimental photo here]

BIBLE VERSE DISCUSSION

Bible Verse of the Week:

(Write a verse here)

_____

_____

_____

What does this verse mean to us?

Dad's thoughts: _____

_____

_____

_____

_____

Son's thoughts: _____

_____

_____

_____

_____

How can we apply this in our daily lives?

_____

_____

_____

_____

_____

_____

_____

_____

[Insert an inspirational photo here]

🚀 FUN ADVENTURE TOGETHER!

📅 **Date:** _____

🎯 **Our Mission Today:**
What exciting thing did we do together?

_____

_____

😃 🎉 **The Best Part:**
What was the most fun or memorable moment?

_____

_____

📷 ✏️ **Picture Time!**
(Draw a picture of our adventure!)

🤝 💙 **Teamwork Moment:**
How did we help each other today?

_____

_____

_____

🙏 👐 **Thank You, God, For:**

One thing we're grateful for today:

_____

_____

🌟 **What We Learned:**

Did we discover something new?

_____

_____

_____

➡️ **Next Adventure Idea:**

What do we want to do together next time?

_____

_____

WEEKLY CHALLENGE

Dad's Challenge for Son: _____

_____

Son's Challenge for Dad: _____

_____

How did we do? (Draw or write about it!)

_____

_____

[Insert a challenge-related photo here]

MEMORY PAGE

This week, we had fun doing _____.

_____

   (Draw or paste a photo here!)

[Insert a memory photo here]

JOKE & RIDDLE CORNER

Dad's joke: _____

_____

_____

Son's joke:

_____

_____

_____

A riddle for next time: _____

_____

_____

[Insert a fun or silly photo here]

STORY TIME

Once upon a time, we went on an adventure...

(Write a story together!)

_____

_____

_____

_____

_____

_____

_____

_____

[Insert an adventure photo here]

GRATITUDE PAGE

Today, I am thankful for...

Dad: _____

Son: _____

[Insert a gratitude-related photo here]

ADVICE FROM DAD

Dad writes a life lesson or advice:

_____

_____

_____

_____

Son writes what he thinks about it:

_____

_____

_____

[Insert a wisdom-themed photo here]

FUTURE MESSAGES

Dad's letter to Son:

_____

_____

_____

_____

Son's letter to Dad:

_____

_____

_____

[Insert a sentimental photo here]

BIBLE VERSE DISCUSSION

Bible Verse of the Week:

(Write a verse here)

_____

_____

_____

What does this verse mean to us?

Dad's thoughts: _____

_____

_____

_____

_____

Son's thoughts: _____

_____

_____

_____

_____

How can we apply this in our daily lives?

_____

_____

_____

_____

_____

_____

_____

_____

[Insert an inspirational photo here]

🚀 FUN ADVENTURE TOGETHER!

📅 **Date:** _____

🎯 **Our Mission Today:**
What exciting thing did we do together?

_____

_____

😃 🎉 **The Best Part:**
What was the most fun or memorable moment?

_____

_____

📷 ✏️ **Picture Time!**
(Draw a picture of our adventure!)

🤝 💙 **Teamwork Moment:**
How did we help each other today?

_____

_____

_____

🙏 🙌 **Thank You, God, For:**

One thing we're grateful for today:

_____

_____

☀️ **What We Learned:**

Did we discover something new?

_____

_____

_____

➡️ **Next Adventure Idea:**

What do we want to do together next time?

_____

_____

WEEKLY CHALLENGE

Dad's Challenge for Son: _____

_____

Son's Challenge for Dad: _____

_____

How did we do? (Draw or write about it!)

_____

_____

[Insert a challenge-related photo here]

MEMORY PAGE

This week, we had fun doing _____.

_____

 (Draw or paste a photo here!)

[Insert a memory photo here]

JOKE & RIDDLE CORNER

Dad's joke: _____

_____

_____

Son's joke:

_____

_____

_____

A riddle for next time: _____

_____

_____

[Insert a fun or silly photo here]

STORY TIME

Once upon a time, we went on an adventure...

(Write a story together!)

_____

_____

_____

_____

_____

_____

_____

_____

[Insert an adventure photo here]

GRATITUDE PAGE

Today, I am thankful for...

Dad: _____

Son: _____

[Insert a gratitude-related photo here]

ADVICE FROM DAD

Dad writes a life lesson or advice:

_____

_____

_____

_____

Son writes what he thinks about it:

_____

_____

_____

[Insert a wisdom-themed photo here]

FUTURE MESSAGES

Dad's letter to Son:

_____

_____

_____

_____

Son's letter to Dad:

_____

_____

_____

[Insert a sentimental photo here]

BIBLE VERSE DISCUSSION

Bible Verse of the Week:

(Write a verse here)

_____

_____

_____

What does this verse mean to us?

Dad's thoughts: _____

_____

_____

_____

_____

Son's thoughts: _____

_____

_____

_____

_____

How can we apply this in our daily lives?

_____

_____

_____

_____

_____

_____

_____

_____

[Insert an inspirational photo here]

🚀 FUN ADVENTURE TOGETHER!

📅 **Date:** _____

🎯 **Our Mission Today:**
What exciting thing did we do together?

_____

_____

😃 🎉 **The Best Part:**
What was the most fun or memorable moment?

_____

_____

📷 ✏️ **Picture Time!**
(Draw a picture of our adventure!)

🤝 💙 **Teamwork Moment:**
How did we help each other today?

_____

_____

_____

🙏 🙌 **Thank You, God, For:**

One thing we're grateful for today:

_____

_____

🌟 **What We Learned:**

Did we discover something new?

_____

_____

_____

➡️ **Next Adventure Idea:**

What do we want to do together next time?

_____

_____

WEEKLY CHALLENGE

Dad's Challenge for Son: _____

_____

Son's Challenge for Dad: _____

_____

How did we do? (Draw or write about it!)

_____

_____

[Insert a challenge-related photo here]

MEMORY PAGE

This week, we had fun doing _____.

_____

   (Draw or paste a photo here!)

[Insert a memory photo here]

JOKE & RIDDLE CORNER

Dad's joke: _____

_____

_____

Son's joke:

_____

_____

_____

A riddle for next time: _____

_____

_____

[Insert a fun or silly photo here]

STORY TIME

Once upon a time, we went on an adventure...

(Write a story together!)

_____

_____

_____

_____

_____

_____

_____

_____

[Insert an adventure photo here]

GRATITUDE PAGE

Today, I am thankful for...

Dad: _____

Son: _____

[Insert a gratitude-related photo here]

ADVICE FROM DAD

Dad writes a life lesson or advice:

_____

_____

_____

_____

Son writes what he thinks about it:

_____

_____

_____

[Insert a wisdom-themed photo here]

FUTURE MESSAGES

Dad's letter to Son:

_____

_____

_____

_____

Son's letter to Dad:

_____

_____

_____

[Insert a sentimental photo here]

BIBLE VERSE DISCUSSION

Bible Verse of the Week:

(Write a verse here)

_____

_____

_____

What does this verse mean to us?

Dad's thoughts: _____

_____

_____

_____

_____

Son's thoughts: _____

_____

_____

_____

_____

How can we apply this in our daily lives?

_____

_____

_____

_____

_____

_____

_____

_____

[Insert an inspirational photo here]

🚀 FUN ADVENTURE TOGETHER!

📅 **Date:** _____

🎯 **Our Mission Today:**
What exciting thing did we do together?

_____

_____

😃 🎉 **The Best Part:**
What was the most fun or memorable moment?

_____

_____

📷 ✏️ **Picture Time!**
(Draw a picture of our adventure!)

🤝 💙 **Teamwork Moment:**
How did we help each other today?

_____

_____

_____

🙏 🙌 **Thank You, God, For:**
One thing we're grateful for today:

_____

_____

☀️ **What We Learned:**
Did we discover something new?

_____

_____

_____

➡️ **Next Adventure Idea:**
What do we want to do together next time?

_____

_____

WEEKLY CHALLENGE

Dad's Challenge for Son: _____

_____

Son's Challenge for Dad: _____

_____

How did we do? (Draw or write about it!)

_____

_____

[Insert a challenge-related photo here]

MEMORY PAGE

This week, we had fun doing _____.

_____

   (Draw or paste a photo here!)

[Insert a memory photo here]

JOKE & RIDDLE CORNER

Dad's joke: _____

_____

_____

Son's joke:

_____

_____

_____

A riddle for next time: _____

_____

_____

[Insert a fun or silly photo here]

STORY TIME

Once upon a time, we went on an adventure...

(Write a story together!)

_____

_____

_____

_____

_____

_____

_____

_____

[Insert an adventure photo here]

GRATITUDE PAGE

Today, I am thankful for...

Dad: _____

Son: _____

[Insert a gratitude-related photo here]

ADVICE FROM DAD

Dad writes a life lesson or advice:

_____

_____

_____

_____

Son writes what he thinks about it:

_____

_____

_____

[Insert a wisdom-themed photo here]

FUTURE MESSAGES

Dad's letter to Son:

_____

_____

_____

_____

Son's letter to Dad:

_____

_____

_____

[Insert a sentimental photo here]

BIBLE VERSE DISCUSSION

Bible Verse of the Week:

(Write a verse here)

_____

_____

_____

What does this verse mean to us?

Dad's thoughts: _____

_____

_____

_____

_____

Son's thoughts: _____

_____

_____

_____

_____

How can we apply this in our daily lives?

_____

_____

_____

_____

_____

_____

_____

_____

[Insert an inspirational photo here]

🚀 FUN ADVENTURE TOGETHER!

📅 **Date:** _____

🎯 **Our Mission Today:**
What exciting thing did we do together?
_____

_____

😃 🎉 **The Best Part:**
What was the most fun or memorable moment?
_____

_____

📷 ✏️ **Picture Time!**
(Draw a picture of our adventure!)

🤝 💙 **Teamwork Moment:**
How did we help each other today?
_____

_____

_____

🙏 👐 **Thank You, God, For:**

One thing we're grateful for today:

_____

_____

☀️ **What We Learned:**

Did we discover something new?

_____

_____

_____

🔜 **Next Adventure Idea:**

What do we want to do together next time?

_____

_____

WEEKLY CHALLENGE

Dad's Challenge for Son: _____

_____

Son's Challenge for Dad: _____

_____

How did we do? (Draw or write about it!)

_____

_____

[Insert a challenge-related photo here]

MEMORY PAGE

This week, we had fun doing _____.

_____

 (Draw or paste a photo here!)

[Insert a memory photo here]

JOKE & RIDDLE CORNER

Dad's joke: _____

_____

_____

Son's joke:

_____

_____

_____

A riddle for next time: _____

_____

_____

[Insert a fun or silly photo here]

STORY TIME

Once upon a time, we went on an adventure...

(Write a story together!)

_____

_____

_____

_____

_____

_____

_____

_____

[Insert an adventure photo here]

GRATITUDE PAGE

Today, I am thankful for...

Dad: _____

Son: _____

[Insert a gratitude-related photo here]

ADVICE FROM DAD

Dad writes a life lesson or advice:

_____

_____

_____

_____

Son writes what he thinks about it:

_____

_____

_____

[Insert a wisdom-themed photo here]

FUTURE MESSAGES

Dad's letter to Son:

_____

_____

_____

_____

Son's letter to Dad:

_____

_____

_____

[Insert a sentimental photo here]

BIBLE VERSE DISCUSSION

Bible Verse of the Week:

(Write a verse here)

_____

_____

_____

What does this verse mean to us?

Dad's thoughts: _____

_____

_____

_____

_____

Son's thoughts: _____

_____

_____

_____

_____

How can we apply this in our daily lives?

_____

_____

_____

_____

_____

_____

_____

_____

[Insert an inspirational photo here]

🚀 FUN ADVENTURE TOGETHER!

📅 **Date:** _____

🎯 **Our Mission Today:**
What exciting thing did we do together?
_____
_____

😃 🎉 **The Best Part:**
What was the most fun or memorable moment?
_____
_____

📷 ✏️ **Picture Time!**
(Draw a picture of our adventure!)

🤝 💙 **Teamwork Moment:**
How did we help each other today?
_____
_____
_____

🙏 🙌 **Thank You, God, For:**
One thing we're grateful for today:

_____

_____

☀️ **What We Learned:**
Did we discover something new?

_____

_____

_____

⏩ **Next Adventure Idea:**
What do we want to do together next time?

_____

_____

WEEKLY CHALLENGE

Dad's Challenge for Son: _____

_____

Son's Challenge for Dad: _____

_____

How did we do? (Draw or write about it!)

_____

_____

[Insert a challenge-related photo here]

MEMORY PAGE

This week, we had fun doing _____ .

_____

   (Draw or paste a photo here!)

[Insert a memory photo here]

JOKE & RIDDLE CORNER

Dad's joke: _____

_____

_____

Son's joke:

_____

_____

_____

A riddle for next time: _____

_____

_____

[Insert a fun or silly photo here]

STORY TIME

Once upon a time, we went on an adventure...

(Write a story together!)

_____

_____

_____

_____

_____

_____

_____

_____

[Insert an adventure photo here]

GRATITUDE PAGE

Today, I am thankful for...

Dad: _____

Son: _____

[Insert a gratitude-related photo here]

ADVICE FROM DAD

Dad writes a life lesson or advice:

_____

_____

_____

_____

Son writes what he thinks about it:

_____

_____

_____

[Insert a wisdom-themed photo here]

FUTURE MESSAGES

Dad's letter to Son:

_____

_____

_____

_____

Son's letter to Dad:

_____

_____

_____

[Insert a sentimental photo here]

BIBLE VERSE DISCUSSION

Bible Verse of the Week:

(Write a verse here)

_____
_____
_____

What does this verse mean to us?

Dad's thoughts: _____

_____
_____
_____
_____

Son's thoughts: _____

_____
_____
_____
_____

How can we apply this in our daily lives?

_____

_____

_____

_____

_____

_____

_____

_____

[Insert an inspirational photo here]

🚀 FUN ADVENTURE TOGETHER!

📅 **Date:** _____

🎯 **Our Mission Today:**
What exciting thing did we do together?
_____
_____

🤪 🎉 **The Best Part:**
What was the most fun or memorable moment?
_____
_____

📷 ✏️ **Picture Time!**
(Draw a picture of our adventure!)

🤝 💙 **Teamwork Moment:**
How did we help each other today?
_____
_____
_____

🙏 👐 Thank You, God, For:
One thing we're grateful for today:

_____

_____

☀️ What We Learned:
Did we discover something new?

_____

_____

_____

🔜 Next Adventure Idea:
What do we want to do together next time?

_____

_____

WEEKLY CHALLENGE

Dad's Challenge for Son: _____

_____

Son's Challenge for Dad: _____

_____

How did we do? (Draw or write about it!)

_____

_____

[Insert a challenge-related photo here]

MEMORY PAGE

This week, we had fun doing _____.

_____

   (Draw or paste a photo here!)

[Insert a memory photo here]

JOKE & RIDDLE CORNER

Dad's joke: _____

_____

_____

Son's joke:

_____

_____

_____

A riddle for next time: _____

_____

_____

[Insert a fun or silly photo here]

STORY TIME

Once upon a time, we went on an adventure...

(Write a story together!)

_____

_____

_____

_____

_____

_____

_____

_____

_____

[Insert an adventure photo here]

GRATITUDE PAGE

Today, I am thankful for...

Dad: _____

Son: _____

[Insert a gratitude-related photo here]

ADVICE FROM DAD

Dad writes a life lesson or advice:

_____

_____

_____

_____

Son writes what he thinks about it:

_____

_____

_____

[Insert a wisdom-themed photo here]

FUTURE MESSAGES

Dad's letter to Son:

_____

_____

_____

_____

Son's letter to Dad:

_____

_____

_____

[Insert a sentimental photo here]

BIBLE VERSE DISCUSSION

Bible Verse of the Week:

(Write a verse here)

_____

_____

_____

What does this verse mean to us?

Dad's thoughts: _____

_____

_____

_____

_____

Son's thoughts: _____

_____

_____

_____

_____

How can we apply this in our daily lives?

_____

_____

_____

_____

_____

_____

_____

_____

[Insert an inspirational photo here]

🚀 FUN ADVENTURE TOGETHER!

📅 **Date:** _____

🎯 **Our Mission Today:**
What exciting thing did we do together?
_____

_____

😃 🎉 **The Best Part:**
What was the most fun or memorable moment?
_____

_____

📷 ✏️ **Picture Time!**
(Draw a picture of our adventure!)

🤝 💙 **Teamwork Moment:**
How did we help each other today?
_____

_____

_____

🙏 👋 **Thank You, God, For:**

One thing we're grateful for today:

_____

_____

🌟 **What We Learned:**

Did we discover something new?

_____

_____

_____

🔜 **Next Adventure Idea:**

What do we want to do together next time?

_____

_____

Made in the USA
Coppell, TX
02 January 2026